Your Story Matters
You Matter

A guide to healing, learning from and sharing your story

Angela Schaefers

Your Story Matters You Matter
A guide to healing, learning from and sharing
your story

Published in the United States by Your Story
Matters Publishing and CreateSpace. First
edition.

ISBN:: 0-9840644-1-9
ISBN-13: 978-0-9840644-1-0

DEDICATION

This book is dedicated to all those, especially E.J. Davis, who never had the opportunity to share their story, but whose lives positively impacted others.

Your story is a gift to share with others!

CONTENTS

Your Story Matters You Matter

About the author, Angela Schaefers

Angela Schaefers is producer and host of Your Story Matters show, a freelance writer and an inspirational speaker. Angela interviews those around the globe who have encouraging and inspiring stories to share. She writes various articles on professional networking, inspiration and why our stories matter. She has authored her memoir Grief to Grace. She is currently working on her next memoir 'More Grace' and an E book 'Cancer Doesn't Come Wrapped In A Pretty Ribbon'. She speaks and shares her story of personal healing, facing stage IV cancer and more to discovering her life purpose. She is a keynote for organizations and events and effectively shares the message within their story. Angela positively impacts the world, one story at a time!

Angela's story~

"In sharing my own life story, I mistakenly believed that no one would want to hear about my story of what I had lived through and have overcome. Yet as I shared my story of living a life of grief to grace, I realized many people wanted and needed to hear about my challenges and the many blessings despite impossible odds. My intention when writing my life story was solely for my children, who at the time were ages 3, 12 and 16. I had been diagnosed with stage IV cancer and was told my life would not last long. Leaving behind my story was a way for my kids to hopefully understand who I was and how I became the person I am through my life experiences. Being encouraged to share my story publicly was life changing! I found great healing through the realization that my story, as just an ordinary person, was something of value to others. When others communicated to me that my story and my survival was one of encouragement, hope and inspiration I felt a sudden, deep in my heart and soul healing. I knew then that all that I endured and overcome was for a reason. Sharing the wisdom I had gained to help others in their life struggles was

amazing. To make such a positive impact on others lives made everything I had been through worth it!"

Having realized the power of her own story to encourage and inspire others and experiencing healing through that, Your Story Matters was created. Angela believes each of our stories have a common thread of hope, courage and faith. A story about a miracle of healing or an unlikely individual succeeding in college to stories about persevering in the midst of a hopeless illness or injury has the ability to encourage and inspire others. Angela has interviewed people from around the globe with encouraging and inspiring stories on subjects such as: discovering the power of determination, surviving domestic violence, facing suicidal thoughts, addiction, successful entrepreneurs, cancer survivors and more! In its first two years Your Story Matters show attracted 83,000 listeners worldwide. Angela regularly hears from listeners who have heard stories that positively impacted them, sometimes to the extent of being life changing.

Angela's profile~

Angela holds a Master of Arts Degree in Counseling from Regent University, and a Bachelor of Arts degree in Organizational Management from Vanguard University. Angela has trained as a Chaplain in Clinical Pastoral Education and is a certified mediator.

Angela provides consulting, coaching and counseling to individuals and small businesses. She has provided counseling to individuals, families, couples and school-aged children. She has provided coaching and consulting to small non-profits and individual business owners. She has provided career coaching to individuals and to groups, including the Los Angeles County Department of Health. She has provided resources, training and speaking as a parent of a special needs child within Florida's early intervention program.

Angela is a mother of three and a mimi (grandmother) to one. She most recently has lived in Florida, prior to living most of her life in California. She is happiest when spending time with her family and closest friends. She enjoys being outdoors, especially at the beach, and likes hiking, biking and kayaking. She is an avid reader, enjoys live music, wine tasting and savors a day at the spa. She has survived cancer for the past nine years and has committed her life to encouraging and inspiring others with her story of survival and living gracefully.

Introduction

When I initially wrote my story, to share with my children, I did so because I had been diagnosed with stage IV cancer and was told I would not have long to live. My children were school-age at the time. I felt compelled to share with them some of my life circumstances and the challenges that I faced because of those circumstances. I wanted them to have a record of me that was straight from my heart about who I was and who I had become. I hoped that after all I had been through that my children would learn from the wisdom I gained through years of living my life. Upon finalizing my story, I asked a couple of close friends to proofread the story for content. They in turn strongly suggested that I create a book about my story and share it with many, not just my children. They believed that my story would help others.

Initially I was very uneasy about that idea! I was very open and honest about my story, beginning from my childhood on. I highlighted the difficulties that were quite personal both to my family and myself. Yet I realized that my story is mine; the good, the bad and the ugly and if there was a possibility that sharing it could benefit just one person, I would have to be courageous and tell it. I do not consider myself a typical writer. I do believe I am a storyteller though! I shared my story in a way that I felt was fitting to who I am. And immediately I had responses from those who read it, such as; "it helped me so much, I appreciate your honesty about the issues you faced, I didn't know someone else has been through what I have, this story inspired and encouraged me like nothing else, thank you for being brave". Suddenly, the most amazing feeling came over me... for the first time in my life I was able to understand that my story, my life, had a bigger purpose then I ever imagined! In spite of all that had occurred, both good and bad, my story has encouraged others, validated others feelings and led many down a path of healing and wholeness through their own stories.

Whatever your reason to share your story, and in whatever way, it is important! Not everyone will choose to share their story publicly, write a book or create a video. Just telling your story will have a powerful impact on others, whether family, friends or to the public. I invite you to leave behind your legacy, because this is what I learned from sharing mine:

~When you share your story with others you put your wisdom to good use

~Telling and sharing your story can change you and others in a positive way

~Your story is your experiences and the circumstances surrounding those experiences... you have a choice to not allow yourself to be a victim of your circumstances

~Everyone's story matters because you are valuable!

May you experience the healing and blessings like I have, from sharing your own story

~ Angela

Why Your Story Matters

Whoever told you that you are not valuable and needed in the world, that you do not have a place and a purpose, lied to you. It is up to you to choose to believe truth vs. the lies. Are you ready?

Most people in the world have been told by others that they are not worthy. Maybe they were told as children and they carried that message within themselves throughout their life. Perhaps they were told as an adult and have lost the once childhood innocence and beauty that all children should grow up with.

With the world constantly evolving into one of instantaneous answers, mass information through the internet, business being done at lightning speed and a less personal mode of communication with others, how do we stay connected to one another? Since the dawn of time story telling has been a powerful and necessary way to pass on information about humanity. Even without the modern day writing tools, stories were told by use of drawings on natural material. Sometimes stories were told simply by what was left behind of a particular group's imprint on the land, man-made tools left behind or even bones. In some cultures, telling stories were passed on from generation to generation and many never died. Through story telling, our very lives have benefitted with knowledge of what worked and didn't work in society. Stories have helped create change over time and preserved cultures that we might have never known about, if not for their story telling.

On an individual level there have been many stories shared about others which have taught wisdom and brought hope and encouragement to others who may believe they cannot overcome certain challenges. We each have had challenges that we have chose to overcome and we have the opportunity to learn from those experiences if we so choose. To go a step further is to share your story with others who may benefit from knowing they are not the only ones who have endured a particular situation and would benefit from the wisdom you gained through your story.

Story telling has been crucial to the growth and changes our world has experienced. Even when evidence of how lives were lived were left behind unintentionally, the gathering of such information helped create a story about how those before us lived. We have learned a great deal about various cultures of the human race from story telling.

Yet, today it seems more and more that the value of telling our story has somehow been lost between technology and the fracture of family and community. When families, neighborhoods and cultures have stories to share about daily life, it helps create a sense of connection. These stories have also helped others to feel encouraged and inspired by what someone has overcome in life and how they have succeeded in various ways.

Nine years ago I would have never imagined the twists and turns my life would take. As a matter of fact, I really did not believe I would be alive today. The only significant thing I had to leave behind for my children was my story. At the time I did not see the real value in my story, not for my children or anyone else. There were many hardships in my childhood, including abuse, a traumatic injury, poverty and homelessness. Although fearful and anxious over what others would think, being encouraged to share my story publicly was life changing! I found great healing through the realization that my story was something of value to others. I knew then that all I endured and had overcome was for a reason. The wisdom I had gained and sharing that wisdom was to help others in their journey of life struggles. To have a positive impact on others lives made everything I have been through worth it!

Initially, I had no intention of putting my story in book format, speaking about it publicly or anything else that has come along since I began this journey. Knowing that my story was making a positive impact on others kept me going. There were many times when I simply did not feel good; I was battling cancer, was a wife, mother and completing my Master's degree. I remember early on I would shake and sweat profusely when standing up to speak and when I went on TV the first time to share my story! I asked myself again and again why I was putting myself through all this. I feel the consistent words of gratitude and encouragement from many saw me through those challenges. I did not have a plan of what would be next, I just fell into circumstances or met people who provided the path to continue on with sharing my story. I have come to believe that sharing my story and others is my life purpose and my intention is to continue to share stories to encourage and inspire many, one story at a time.

The more I have shared about my story and others stories, the more interested people are in hearing more about my life and other's experiences, and how I and others handle challenging circumstances. I am often asked for advice, counsel, and words of encouragement from those who are suffering similar challenges I have suffered in the past, or am currently facing. It has proven to me how powerful sharing what we have learned from our story can be to help others.

I have shared my story through my first book Grief to Grace, through public speaking at community events, service groups, young adult groups and interviews on local cable shows in both Los Angeles and Tampa. I also shared my story on my own show Your Story Matters, and when I am interviewing others about their stories I draw on my own part of my story that fits along their subject matter. I continue to share my story through blogging and written articles. For me, personally sharing my story is a valuable way to leave behind a legacy that matters and make a difference in others lives.

I think that if you decide to tell your story you should first be willing to learn from it. The power in your story is in the wisdom you have gained from your experiences. You may not always see what exactly your story does to encourage, enlighten or inspire others. But that does not mean it has not had a positive impact. However, if your mission in sharing your story is to gain attention or pity it may mean that you have not healed the wounds of the past. Each of us do things for our own reasons, and I have shared my reasons as to why I am on this journey to share my story and other's stories. It may be important for you to determine what your reason is.

The following questions are designed for you to determine why you may want to share your story:

What are some of the topics of stories you have heard that caused you to reflect on changing and personal growth?

What type of stories have you heard that creating a feeling of being encouraged or inspired?

Have you ever overcome a situation, challenge or circumstance that you were able to learn something from?

If you knew that sharing what you have endured and overcome would help someone else to realize there is hope and that they can get through what they are facing, would you feel your story is valuable?

Have you ever dealt with being abused (physically or emotionally), suffering an illness, having a life-long dream come true, succeeding as an athlete, artist or musician? Perhaps you are a single parent or you live with a disability or have a family member with one. Or have you faced death, divorce, a career change, or a cross country move? There are so many things that we deal with in life and each of them shape us in different ways.

How have your life experiences (good and bad) shaped you as a person, both positively and negatively?

Have you had positive experiences during your story that taught you the goodness of others and the power of happiness?

I believe that you can find the answer as to why your story matters via the previous questions. Often we do not think whatever we have lived through or experienced would matter much to anyone else or make a difference in their life. I cannot express how untrue that is! Not only have I experienced the power in sharing my story to touch others, but many others have learned the power in sharing theirs too! We are all valuable and necessary in this world. Collectively we make it the amazing and miraculous world that it is. My question is, why not share with one another, those little stories and big stories that offer wisdom and insight?

Defining The Message Within Your Story

~Telling your story can be freeing, especially when it's been hidden away for so long

~Telling your story can help you to understand what you've learned from your experiences

~Telling your story can help you to realize how your experiences both shaped and impacted you as a person

~Telling your story can help you to recognize your life purpose based on what you have overcome and achieved through difficulties

~Sharing your story with others often creates a shared connection of human emotion that will encourage understanding and compassion for humanity individually and as a whole

~Things you've learned along the way can help someone else who may have experienced something similar but feels lost in their circumstances

~Sharing your story can empower you and give hope to others

The following reflective questions are presented as a tool to begin contemplating your story and what it means to you and may mean to others. There are no right or wrong answers, nor is it necessary to feel like you have to be a "writer" or have any story other than your very own to share!

What are some of your personal stories you often share with others, that are either from your past or more recently?

What is it about these stories that compel you to share it with others? (What's the main message?)

Are there stories that you think about at times, but that you do not share with others? If so, what are the topics of these stories?

If these stories are thought about but not shared, what is the reason you are not sharing them?

Whether you have stories you have shared or not shared, what are some of the things you have learned when reflecting on your story?

(For example you may have learned why you feel a certain way about something or you have learned things to do or not do based on experience)

How has your story (experiences) played a role in who you are?

(For example if you have been or are a part of the military how has that experience affected you and how you live life?)

What achievements have you made or obstacles have you overcome despite the difficulties you faced in your story?

What stories have you been told/heard that have created understanding and compassion for fellow humans? (An example may be someone suffering physically and their determination to achieve success)

Whether your story is about life's "typical" situations or a significant experience, is it possible that it too will help someone else to have understanding or compassion for others? Or maybe it will give someone else the skills necessary to deal with their own situation? If so, how?

What are some of the ways that you communicate your likes and dislikes or the ways you feel best communicating?

(For example; writing stories, writing poetry, art, music, dance)

I realized during my own healing process and defning the message within my story that I felt lost, confused and sometimes bewildered by my own story. It took talking it through with others, reading how others overcame their life challenges, and learning from those around me who were emotionally healthy to sort through the many emotions and memories. Once things became more clear, I was able to truly learn from my story. Have you ever felt lost in the circumstances of your life situation and if so, how did you get through those difficulties? You may think you have not overcome as much as you have. Again, not everyone will suffer abuse, loss or other significant life challenges. But we all go through changes and life happenings. We all learn along the way how to handle whatever happens and create ways to react and repsond to both good and bad experiences. The way you handle things is a big key to understanding how your story defines you.

Healing and Learning From Your Story

Should you decide to share your story or not, reflecting, learning and healing from it will be valuable to you. Understanding your experiences, which is your story, will help you to realize how your story has both shaped and impacted you as a person. Often when we reflect on our story we can began to see the patterns of our lives, the journey becomes clearer and the learning can lead to discovering your destiny and purpose.

The following questions provide an overview of some of the things I have personally asked myself and worked through finding the answers. It helped me to understand who I am and what my life purpose is. Each of us have our own journey, although we may experience similar circumstances, challenges and obstacles. There are always differences in how life affects us and how we deal with it. No story is the same nor is the outcome of a story.

Though painful to answer at times, asking myself these questions, and being completely honest with myself, I learned a great deal about life. I learned that my experiences with loneliness, shame, dysfunctional relationships, and poverty collectively lead me to sabotaging my own peace of mind and happiness. These experiences also deterred me from being able to trust myself and others. On some level it seems each of us as humans have experienced a lot of the same things, but to varying degrees. I have included reflective questions so that you may be able to determine if any of these things were or are a part of your story and require healing from. Please remember that you have your own experiences and feelings and they will not match mine or anyone else's in the universe exactly.

Often it is not easy to face our past. There are many emotions that may surface when you begin to think about your story. You may feel uncomfortable, challenged, defensive and possibly unwilling to be completely honest with yourself. I realize that sharing my own story and asking you reflective questions about your story may be far from enough for you to begin or complete your healing process. It certainly was not a quick or easy process for me to heal and I did not do it alone! I had trusted friends, family and professional counselors at times to support, guide or encourage me and I advise you to do the same. I do not believe that any of us were put on earth to endure, live or celebrate life alone. If you do not have people in your life that you are close to and can trust it will help if you find a pastor, counselor or support group to share with.

I understand and have lived in the place of shame and believed for years that if others knew my story they would be appalled. It was as if the humiliation I felt and endured during childhood seeped from my pores. I believe the biggest deterrent to my healing many years ago was the deeply imbedded shame and guilt I felt. I lived with a false knowledge of feeling responsible for every bad thing that ever happened to me or around me. If your shame is this deep I suggest you write down all your shameful experiences from as early as you can remember. Once the list is completed, go through it and cross off everything that was not in your control. Whatever is left are things you will need to face, learn to let go of and forgive yourself for. There will undoubtedly be things in your life and perhaps people that will require forgiveness. Please do not let your shame or guilt over things deter you from your healing process, or (if you are so inclined) from sharing your story!

It's important to understand that your story does NOT need to be about tragedy and to know that part of your story can be very much indirectly related to you. Having a good childhood and life is great and happens often! There is learning in that too! The questions to reflect on will be appropriate to both negative and positive emotions that you have had along your journey. You could also have had a family member whose story greatly impacted yours. Perhaps there was a significant death in your circle of life, or a parent was absent or had an addiction. Perhaps you had a sibling or parent that had a medical condition that greatly impacted you. Any and all of these things impact your story.

We learn about life through our experiences. How we respond and handle our life experiences has a great deal to do with our environment and the influences around us. Changing how we typically respond to life circumstances can be done and is necessary when your usual reactions and responses are not the best choices to make. It personally took me years to understand that a) there were other ways to respond/react than what I had been taught or observed and b) I had a choice!

When you think back to your childhood, do you feel it was a happy, sad or indifferent time of your life? For many years I never thought about my childhood as being 'bad' or any different than others. Sometimes it takes time and reflection to remember our past and put it into perspective.

Were there experiences during your childhood that created feelings of fear, shame, guilt or other negative emotions? If so, please list. Sometimes these things are not easy to admit or face. Sometimes these emotions are confusing, one sign is when a memory or experience makes you feel uncomfortable but you are not sure why. Often that is a clue that reflection is needed.

Were there experiences during your childhood when you felt happy, love and fulfilled? If so, please list. You may think that there are way too many to list (that's great!). This could also be the case with the question flipped as above to be about the negative (not so great).

Again, these questions and the reflection back into the past can create a great deal of emotions, both positive and negative. A good tip is to limit your responses. The key is to focus on what comes to mind first and/or what memories you have remembered over time, talked about over time or that have had a significant impact on you.

A very helpful way to begin organizing your thoughts and learn from your story is by making a side by side list. On one side, write down the experience you had and on the other write down the emotion connected to that. *This should be limited to a few words. For example:

__EXPERIENCE__	__EMOTION__
Going out for ice cream with my dad	Felt loved and special
Being told you are never going to amount to anything	Felt humiliated and shamed

Once you have completed your side by side list, look for what experiences and emotions are most significant to you. Look for

51

repeated examples of a particular emotion that has come up more than others. *Remember in doing this exercise that blaming others or making every emotion and experience about others is not the point. The experience may be about a family member experiencing something or impacting you by their situation, but your emotion is yours.

Hopefully at this point you are beginning to hone in on your story, the most impactful parts of it. Next is the learning part about how our story affected who you are, and what parts may or may not need to heal while connecting to your life purpose.

When I looked back on my own story, I realized (after I was able to face the reality of both the circumstances, my actions and those of others) that there were a few things that repeated over time. A few examples;

Shame ~ I remember early on feeling ashamed and guilty on a regular basis, because of other's demeaning words and/or disappointing looks. My story told me that I was more inclined to feel a deeper sense of having no value as a person because of what others said about me OR because they did not express positive and healthy love and acceptance towards me.

Caring For Others ~ Though I learned as an adult that I often took care of others and tried to please them for all the wrong reasons, I also learned that something within me felt compelled to care for others and to help with no expectations in return. Once I resolved my heart issues of feeling it necessary to gain others acceptance, the core of my nature, that of being giving, loving and kind emerged more significantly.

When I made my list of experiences and the emotions attached I saw that there were several varying experiences creating the same emotion (ex. shame). And then there were many experiences where I felt useful, valuable, helpful etc. that really lead me to the word 'caring' to describe myself. After reflection and looking over the list more than once, I saw that though my life had its share of highs, lows and chaos there was a theme in how collectively it all impacted me and who I became.

53

I took the time to sort through my experiences (my story) to learn about how I perceived things, why I reacted to certain things and people the way I did, and who I had become from all this. I was able to sort through many, many feelings from years of living out my story. From my story I learned about:

- Love
- Fear
- Shame
- Why people are the way 'they' are
- Blame vs. taking responsibility

The next chapter will walk you through discovering your unique purpose and value in this world!

Discover Your Purpose
Through Your Story

Your story reveals your purpose. The greatest of story tellers find a way to reveal a *truth* or *message* in the stories they tell. Maya Angelou is a great story teller, who can tell a story she created from imagination or one about her own life, and do so poignantly. From our favorite childhood tales to the greatest literary stories, the best are those with messages that stir us down to our cores to feel encouraged and inspired.

We are not all story tellers, but we each have our own story that has an important message within it. Our story is important because we are important. Some of our stories are laced with experiences of joy and excitement and others with tragedy and turmoil. Many fit in the middle of those two extremes. Each of our stories are a part of who we are and play a role in shaping us.

The theme of our story is based on what we have learned and experienced over time. Patterns develop from both our positive and negative life circumstances. The need to be mentally strong to endure physically or emotionally creates certain behaviors. Living with few challenges and a stable environment often require less self sufficiency. In either case, the patterns we live by and the habits we form create a theme.

When we learn how our story has affected and impacted us, we can then begin to better understand who we are. If we have suffered the impacts of emotional and physical pain or abuse, perhaps we have developed an attitude of bitterness. If we have lived a life wherein we felt happy, loved, and supported perhaps we have developed an attitude of joy. Many people have experienced a variety of experiences during their life journey which creates a balanced attitude, while others have not.

You may believe that your story has been weighted heavily towards good or bad, yet evidence suggests that everyone endures both positive and negative experiences from childhood on. It is often our perception, based on our experiences, that creates a mindset about our story. That mindset must be explored to find the meaning in our story.

Look over the following keys to finding your purpose through your story and write down your thoughts about each.

1) Look back at a recorded history of your story: videos, photos and written word, and find those experiences that you learned the most from

2) Consider the many things you have learned from your story and pick the top 5 things that have empowered you to be a better person

3) Look for patterns throughout your story, of those times in your life, when you felt deeply passionate and driven about something, whether to get through an obstacle you faced or being deeply affected by something/someone

4) Consider input from others throughout your story to determine if any words of affirmation you received align with who you are, based on what you have experienced

5) Put together your passions, affirmations received, and your unique abilities to see that you are the star role of your story, that is in itself your individual purpose (for example: I like to help others, I have been told that I am good at listening, supporting and encouraging others. I have a special ability to see the core of other's problems and offer workable solutions for them to move forward. Through the trials and tragedies of my life, I have maintained my ability to love and care for others. As I have healed from my past, I have refined my role as counselor.)

We each have a unique purpose here on earth, one that when we recognize and live it makes us a superstar! If you have ever felt that you are not a superstar, you don't deserve to shine or to be recognized for your leading role, then perhaps you should revisit your story to see the amazing within you! Don't let others be the only superstars, claim your fame!

"We delight in the beauty of the butterfly, but rarely admit the changes it has gone through to achieve that beauty." ~ Maya Angelou

Their Story Matters
Your Story Matters

You may, or may not know of some of the following people. They have had the courage to share their story and had a positive impact on others by doing so.

~ Maya Angelou

~ Dave Pelzer

~ Temple Grandin

~ Chris Gardner

~ Ishmael Beah

~ Leo Buscaglia

~ Randy Pausch

~ Henri J.M. Nouwen

~ Dale Evans Rogers

~ Frederick Buechner

~ Harold S. Kushner

There are so many others; this is only a very small list. The list is eclectic and the stories will touch some more than others or be easy to relate to for some more than others. The point is, these are normal people, like you and I, who had a story to tell and told it. Collectively these stories are about human life: suffering, accomplishments, love, and leaving a legacy behind.

Hearing a story of courage, hope and perseverance can create positive change in others. Sharing our story, specifically what we have learned on our journey, can bring hope to the hopeless. The following are snippets of stories about people who have overcome challenges and have shared their stories on Your Story Matters show. Your Story Matters show was created to share a variety of stories on many topics without limiting the shows to gender, race, or location. The stories from around the globe are all about the power of the human spirit, which in itself is not limiting. It is only our sometimes limited beliefs that we are not the same while being different.

Sharron is a God-fearing woman whose dream was to marry and have a family. She recounts singing in the church choir and feeling like a hypocrite knowing that all was not well within her own family due to her son's drug addiction. Many years into dealing with the pain and shame of her family secret, Sharron decided to go public with her story to help others to have hope and faith amidst their circumstances. More information can be found at http://efamilyrecovery.com/

Rajesh is a successful IT professional who had both legs and one arm amputated as a child. Rajesh shares his story of obstacles and challenges he faced throughout his life because of being different. Rajesh felt called to do more with his life and has since trained and become a triathlete. He is using his platform to encourage other amputees to become athletes and to assist and connect with others to develop high-functioning prosthesis for athletes. He has completed the Ironman Kona. More information can be found at http://www.live-free.net/

Randi was a counselor and special needs teacher when she became ill with a brain tumor. Being told she would not survive and not being able to continue teaching due to liability issues, she started to bake and share her treats. She went on to create a successful business of homemade, healthy desserts and won the Best First Cookbook in the World 2004 award. Randi continues to share her recipes with others, including writing another cook specific to healthy eating for children. More information can be found at http://www.themuffinlady.com

Reed was a successful professional in the non-profit sector prior to being laid off. He decided to make a commitment of one year of giving $10 a day to random individuals. He did so in honor of his mother who had passed away, and had instilled in him a heart of altruism. Reed has touched the lives of many and set an example of giving by tracking and sharing his daily giving experiences. More information can be found at http://yearofgiving.org/

The topics covered, so far, on Your Story Matters show include:

- Cancer survival
- Living with spina bifida

- Surviving being a Cambodian refugee and creating a successful new life
- Suicide
- Addiction
- Financial success
- Physical healing after surgery, accident or disease
- Spiritual healing
- Surviving domestic violence
- Non-profit organizations creating change
- Successful entrepreneurs who overcame obstacles and did not give up and more!

You may subscribe to iTunes to get the latest show each week and you can find the archived shows at www.yourstorymatters.net. The shows are interviews of courageous people, who have not only overcome challenges and obstacles but who also are sharing a part of their story to help others!

There are many more stories from all over the world that can inspire us. Each of our stories has the possibility of creating positive change in others by encouraging and inspiring them! You may think that your story does not equate to any of the stories above. You may think that your 'challenge' or 'tragedy' is not valuable enough for you to share. You may mistakenly believe that nothing in your story could possibly encourage or inspire others.

If you have not learned from the nuggets of wisdom from your own story and have not shared that wisdom, how do you know that your story does not matter? How do you know that a random stranger may be encouraged to stop doing something harmful to themselves or others after hearing your story? How do you know that someone feeling hopeless and suicidal won't find hope in hearing about your story of overcoming obstacles and challenges? How do you know that someone who hears your story may for once in their life feel they too are lovable, despite their flaws and mistakes made?

You do not know. And what if just one person were positively impacted by your story? What if your story changed a life for the better? What if your story saved a life? What if your story impacted MANY? Would you be willing to share your story then? Would you be willing to be a part of the Your Story Matters. You Matter. movement, changing the world one story at a time?

It's important to think about what stories have had a positive impact on you and why. It is just as important to reflect on what you learned from these stories. And then you may begin to connect how your own story has value too!

Sometimes people are forever changed by hearing someone else's story of survival. Sometimes someone will literally forgo attempting suicide or take a step to get help for their problems. All because they heard a story from someone like them or in a similar situation. It happens often. And yet, what if there were no stories for others to learn from? What if we all walked through life feeling our story was not worthy of sharing and did not matter? I want to share this true account of an experience I had one day and the letter I received later.

Dear Ms. Angela,

I do not know if you remember me. I met you that one day when you caught me outside in the corner of the office building. You mistakenly came back there, I thought at the time, but now I know it was like God was sending me an angel.

I thought you were crazy and yet I was the crazy one, smoking crack on my lunch break, 200 feet from my office. Someone else would have jumped out of their skin the way I snapped at you, asking you what you wanted and being too stoned to realize you were not trying to spy on me! Not you, you just smiled and walked away.

Then the really crazy part happened. I was so relieved that you were gone and I could go back to smoking before my lunch break was over. But there you were. Smiling. Again.

And you handed me your card as I snarled at you and asked you if you were judging me. Then you said "no sister, I just want to give you this hope card and let you know there is hope for you too". I was dumb founded, but inside I was so ashamed because you were kind and I was horrible.

You turned and walked away and I honestly thought I must be really high to have imagined some crazy woman spying on me and giving me some stupid card. But a few days later I found the card. It said H.O.P.E. is having the opportunity to provide encouragement. I laughed and thought, that will never be me. Who in the hell would I ever encourage?

I went to the website on the card. There you were. Smiling. Again. I listened to a lot of those stories and something happened to me deep down. I knew I had to change. I knew I had to get help. I knew, like some of the people in the stories that I could do better. I am working on it. I wanted to tell you that and to thank you.

RS

The greatest gift I have ever received is that of knowing that people are encouraged and inspired by my story or someone else's that I have helped to share. I have had many messages from people around the globe who have said that the stories on Your Story Matters show have encouraged or inspired them to: get help, attempt to change, believe in themselves, have hope, discover their own faith and more! This feedback has confirmed that sharing our stories, whatever it may be about, has the potential to have a positive impact on others! It has also confirmed that our stories are what connect us as a human race. Not one person I have heard from has mentioned anything about someone's gender, race or where they come from. That is not relevant when we realize that we all have potential to learn from our stories and become better people and encourage that in those around us!

Why You Matter

Have you ever wondered why you matter? Or have you found yourself not even questioning why you matter, because you *never* believed you mattered? I personally have felt and questioned both. For so long, I never knew that the world would be any different with me in it or not. My story of origin includes various feelings of self-loathing, shame, guilt and fear. All combined, I honestly felt that I was not *worthy* of anything; a good life, love, peace. I did not understand what self-love was nor did I feel what it was like to be 'comfortable' in my own skin.

Since I have discovered the beauty within and the value of 'me', I have realized that many, many people do not think they matter. They simply exist, feeling as though they are a burden, not important in the big scheme of the world or life in general. Perhaps because I remember that painful and lonely existence, I truly feel for those in that place of their lives. Some people have been living there for years. Some have never experienced that feeling of knowing that they are valuable and a necessary part of this world.

That to me, is one of the biggest shames ever, that people are not valued. That often 'things', money or even places are more valuable and coveted than human beings. Part of the mission of *Your Story Matters* is to strive towards a world where each of us know we are valuable and necessary. Better yet, that we would each have self-love and know we are lovable. Yes, flaws and all, imperfections physically, and having made mistakes too.

I can share with you why I feel you matter. In fact I will give you a list of 33 reasons why, below. Yet, the truth is, until YOU believe you matter, you will never believe it coming from a motivational speaker, reading an inspiring book or seeing an uplifting video. Because you see, all those things are all around us, if we choose to see and partake in them. And even then we must be able to take these things in, within the depths of our soul. We have to live in that place of *knowing* that we matter, that we are lovable, and that what we bring to this world is necessary.

What will it take for you to feel that you matter? For you to know that your life is valuable and necessary in this world?

Some of you may need to heal from the past. Some of you, like me, may have been abused, abandoned, and neglected. Or maybe you were shamed to your core, all creating a sense of no self-worth, no self-love and zero value. **Despite whatever happened in your story to create a sense of worthlessness in you, the truth is that you have the option to choose to HEAL and to think and feel differently than what your experiences instilled in you!**

Will you make the choice to NOT be a victim of your circumstances? To learn to love and value YOU and to be the best part of this world that you can be? Will you make a choice to learn from your story and use that learning to be a better person and to share your wisdom with others?

If you are still asking 'how' that is okay. Go back to Chapter 4, Healing From Your Story.

- Think about the reflective questions
- Journal
- Seek counsel
- Ask someone close and trusted to work through your thoughts with you

Just don't give up. Because healing is possible and available to each of us. It is one of the gifts of the universe.

33 Reasons Why You Matter

1. You were brought into this world for a purpose; your purpose is different than any others and is important

2. Others need you~ family, friends, random people along the journey

3. Your whole being is unique to the world; your looks, your voice, your touch, your ability to love

4. You have taught others something, whether big or small they know something more because of you

5. You are part of the world going round; life is a circular event, starting with the creation of human beings

6. You have been/are the object of someone's affection

7. You have brought a smile to someone

8. You have given affection to someone

9. Your words have made a difference in someone's life

10. Your unique talents and gifts are part of something created (again could be small, big or seemingly insignificant)

11. Your actions have helped others

12. You have helped others by listening to them

13. You have helped others by caring

14. You gave someone a reason to live

15. You gave someone a reason to hope

16. You gave someone a reason to strive towards being better

17. Your words were part of a conversation that needed your voice

18. Sometime during your life you were the last person needed to: make a full team, balance the weight on the boat or eat the last part of the meal

19. You are a friend

20. You are a family member to someone

21. You have made a difference in the world simply by being you

22. You have created something unique to you (even if it was your secret chili recipe or that sandwich that others don't ask what's in it)

23. Something you wrote, art you created, or music you made had an impact on others
24. You have made someone's heart flutter

25. You have made someone else think differently

26. You have given someone goose bumps

27. You have encouraged someone

28. You learned something from a teacher

29. You read something, played a song or looked at art that someone created

30. You taught someone about love

31. You taught someone about life

32. You helped someone in some small way that mattered (holding a door, giving up your seat)

33. You shared a part of you with others

The Story Continues

While I admit that when I originally wrote my life story, 'Grief to Grace', it was truly what I thought would be the end of my life. I did not consider writing the ending in an open-ended way because it was meant to be my final thoughts. Having been blessed to live beyond my diagnosis, currently nine years, I have realized that the story continues for many of us. Regardless of when you share your story or even what part of your story you emphasize, there is more.

While I think it is important to capture the main message of your story, which many times leads to your life purpose, life can change drastically over time and much more can be 'added' to your story. I am sure there are even instances where a new chapter in life, or a new season as some say, could bring about a completely different perspective on what your purpose is. We certainly are creatures of great depth, multi-faceted and unique.

Though I believe at this point that my story has lead me to my purpose of sharing my own and other's stories, I also feel that I have lived several different lives over the years and perhaps there are a few more to come. By that I mean our environment, career, relationships can greatly impact the life we live. Who knows what lies ahead?

Part of what I learned since being diagnosed with cancer is that life and death are vicarious. We simply do not have any absolutes in either case. Learning to be in a place of acceptance about whatever we cannot change or what the future holds can be very freeing. At the same time keeping our hearts and minds open to learning as our story continues to unfold is important too.

I have also learned that many times while we are in the midst of our life story, it is challenging to track what is happening, what learning opportunities there are and what matters most in our story. At times it may not be possible to capture the importance of what is happening in your story. For instance, when you are grieving, dealing with treatment for a life-threatening disease or facing divorce that is normal. I have had a few life events happen since my cancer diagnosis and I felt like I was just washed under a huge wave that took a bit of time to come out from under. I could only process certain events after the fact.

Then I knew there was healing to be done. And this is where you can find the value in your own story. For me, part of healing: letting go, acceptance, and moving on requires learning. Learning from what happened, not necessarily why, but how. How did I get in this situation, and how did life go from this to that? Learning about my reactions to life circumstances and about the emotions stemming from them helped me to put whatever I went through into perspective. I could then accept responsibility for my part, have empathy for others that may have hurt me, and find peace in some circumstances that were simply life happening.

In the learning I found valuable pieces of my story. Just during the past nine years I learned:

- Acceptance of a disease that I had no control over, but to take charge of my day to day life
- Letting go of relationships can be painful but necessary for all involved, for various reasons
- My life purpose isn't something I am striving to get to, like the pot at the end of the rainbow, but is a way to live each day
- Part of being a good parent was learning to let go of control and love more, while trusting the process for my children's lives
- Peace is available to me in any circumstance as long as I stay present in all that I am blessed with here and now
- Today is enough; if I do not make it past today I am okay with who I am, what I have accomplished, and anything left on my 'to do list'
- Other's reactions when they are affected negatively by someone else's story (disease, death, divorce) is about them and not my responsibility
- Letting go of love is not easy and hurts deeply, but love comes in many forms and will come back again
- Everyday I have the opportunity to start fresh, to wake up and be grateful that I am alive for today, forget yesterday and not worry about tomorrow

Of course these are just the highlights of the past nine years. But these are the things that have impacted me the most. They provide learning from my story so that I can in turn share with others to encourage and inspire them.

The key for you is to occasionally ask yourself what has been happening in your life that you need to heal from or learn from? Then you can share that wisdom with others. The gift in life is that our story is powerful and meaningful, and it really does not matter if your story is like mine or not, it will speak to someone. Everyone has a story based on their experiences.

You never know who will value from learning about your challenges or triumphs. The person you least expect, a family member or a random stranger can hear a part of your story and it could very well change their life. How will you know if you do not share it? Too many people tell me that their story does not matter. They say "nothing that bad has happened" or "nothing that amazing has happened", which I say, "isn't our perspective simply that? Ours, not other's". How do you know that someone else doesn't want or need your insight and your wisdom about something?

I am not saying that we all need to write a book or walk around everyday telling our story. I am simply asking that you consider the learning parts of your story and that you remain open to sharing that with others as necessary. This of course requires community, talking and sharing with others. And that of course includes some level of trust. Perhaps sometimes we have to trust that what we say and share will have a positive impact and is giving a gift.

When we give a gift, we do not assume that the receiver will hate it or reject it. We assume that they will graciously accept it at the very minimum. We may have an expectation that someone's response will be a happy one, or worse yet, hope they will be impressed by our gift. Or we can simply give freely. No expectations. In some cases we may never be thanked for that gift or know that it meant something to someone. And that is how I have found a lot of stories, when shared, are. They are gifts, sometimes life changing. And yet depending on how, when, and to whom you share them with who knows the outcome? If there is a chance, even in the slightest, to encourage and inspire others or teach them something of value, isn't it worth it?

So You Want To Share Your Story? (HOORAY!)

Everyone has a story worth telling. Some of us will tell that story through music, art or poetry or writing in book, blog, or article format. If you feel compelled to share the message in your story, I invite you to consider the following questions:

1) Are you willing to shorten or lengthen what you have written or recorded in order to create a clear and concise message, if necessary?

2) If you would like to capture your message in video, art or music form do you have prior experience in that? (if not you can utilize the services/help of others)

3) What outcome do you expect from sharing your message? (personally, professionally, & financially)

4) What budget have you set to create the book/video/art etc?

5) Where/who is your target audience? (i.e.- religious/spiritual groups, elderly, ill, locally, globally, virtually etc)

6) What is your time frame? (what date to start the project, what date to be mid-point and what date to have the finished product)

7) What can you realistically commit to in promoting, sharing & selling the project (time, energy, finding resources)?

8) Will you be creating additional projects in the future via writing, art, or film?

9) Have you considered a workbook format for your book, an E book, a video series, an illustrated book, a series of art?

10) What do you see as being the core of your message? (1-3 sentences)

11) What problem will your message solve, questions will your message answer or change will your message promote? (1-3 sentences)

My Personal Tips For Sharing Your Message-

• Find like-minded individuals who are sharing & supporting a similar message (i.e. if your message is about domestic violence, find local and national DV groups/organizations)

• Create and memorize a 3-5 minute statement that clearly communicates your message (this should be very clear and easy for others to understand)

• Use your statement via social media & when you are around others who may ask what you do

• Create a business card that shares a powerful word or two about your message & your easiest contact info (email, phone or web site)

• Give a copy of your book, audio or other material to local business owners who may be inclined to share your message and/or allow you to speak, do a book signing etc. - again choose places & people who make sense for you to connect with- (i.e. a hospital if perhaps your message is related to illness/disease)

- Follow-up... ALWAYS! Even if you have met someone randomly who is not in your 'field' or have any connection to your message, they may connect you to someone who is and does (this includes online connections)

- Create an easy way for others to buy your product/service (website, facebook, local business)

- Think outside the box by asking your local providers to sell your product or post your business card/ flyer etc. (especially those directly connected to your message- for instance, your doctor if your message is about health or perhaps your local grocery store if you sell a grocery store item)

- Ask your closest friends/colleagues/supporters to carry around your product or perhaps a post card size flyer to share with those they come across who may be in need of your service/product

- Check into your local government entities to inquire about sharing your message or posting info (for instance- local library, parks & recreation etc)

- Donate your product to an organization that would benefit from it

- Utilize local entities such as local and global cable shows, radio shows, newspapers etc. to share your message (ask to be on air, be interviewed, write an article etc.)

- Wear a name badge at meetings/events, a shirt with your business name etc in public, often

- Purchase an affordable marketing product to put your name (or business name) on and give out accordingly- for instance: pens, note pads etc

- Whatever you are sharing to draw people to your product or service should be consistent (i.e. post cards, pens, inside your book, your biz card etc. should have the same link or to find you/your product/service)

- Consider the best way for YOU to connect, respond and build relationships- is it via social media, telephone, or face-to-face? Utilize that way the most, so it is easier for you to follow up and connect

- Find a blog, web page or facebook page that is like minded and comment on their posts (i.e. a coach finds other coach's, counselors etc.) blogs that you can share at & at the same time create more networking with like-minded individuals/groups

- Find and utilize others to help with things you are not experienced at (ex. writing marketing material, technical support for Facebook, blogging etc.)

- Find others to support & encourage your endeavors (someone you can share your frustrations, questions, & successes with)

I have learned:

- There is a continual need to re-evaluate my message, approach, and efforts to make changes accordingly when I find something is not working for me (ex: I used to do group emails and little response came back and I've changed my business cards and web page periodically to create more interest)

- I have to be my #1 promoter and be consistent in promoting my cause (I was surprised at how the momentum in my followers and interest began to wane when I was not consistent at keeping in contact with others)

- When I connect others (which is something I love to do because I love to help others) it also creates more connections for me

- Some people are willing to help me or support me as long as I do something for them (ex. buy their product or service) and I do not operate that way. I will help share messages and encourage others to utilize a business or service if I believe in it, but I can also support it without hesitation even if they do nothing for me

- I had to make a decision along this journey as to how much time and energy I could realistically put into what I do and look at how it fits into my priorities (again, if time is an issue then you need to decide how to proceed)

- I had to make a decision on how much money I wanted to invest in what I am doing while knowing that I cannot guarantee the return on my investment (recently I decided to no longer pay to join groups or pay to go to seminars etc)

- I had to look at the return on my investment of time & money and determine if what I was doing was creating the end result that I desired (For me the ultimate result is encouraging & inspiring others)

- I have learned to be cautious & thoughtful with the many requests to 'partner up' or utilize a service (such as a PR firm) and always go back to my core values & my mission

- I have learned that many people mean well when expressing support and/or excitement to do projects together but mostly do not have the ability to follow through. (It could be financial issues, time available, or being unrealistic in what they thought they could do)

- I have learned that being consistent has been the #1 reason for the following and/or interest in me (this is not the same as new products, services or ideas)

- I have learned to watch and listen to what others like, pay attention to or show interest in

- Many people will be happy to have me speak, write for or provide product for free, and that does help spread my message. But I learned to be discerning in what I give/provide so that I know it makes sense for me and does not take away time & energy where I need to focus it

- I learned to be specific about my "why" (I suggest you read Simon Sinek's 'Start With Why') and to live my why day in and day out- it keeps me focused!

The Journey From Grief to Grace to Your Story Matters

The past six years on my journey, starting out with Grief to Grace, have been an amazing and blessed one for sure. I have included a history of the journey for those interested but at the same time, I hope to encourage others to follow their dreams. Most importantly, to follow their hearts.

As previously mentioned, I initially wrote my story for my children as a way to share my life experiences and how they shaped who I was. At the time, I had recently been told that I had stage IV terminal cancer and I was advised to get my final matters in order. I felt compelled to leave something for my children to go back to, when they were old enough, in order to have a better understanding of who their mom was. When I finished writing my story I had a couple of close friends proofread it for content. They felt that my story was powerful and worth sharing with others. I will be forever grateful for those first gentle pushes of encouragement to begin this adventure!

It took a bit for me to accept that I should share my story with others. I really believed that my story was not of much importance to anyone else. I could not imagine many people wanting to read it. As I thought through this endeavor and prayed for wisdom and guidance, things began to unfold and a book became a reality I never expected. From a close friend who is an artist who designed my first book cover, to an impromptu seminar with Time Warner's publishing division, to opportunities to speak, do book signings and be interviewed on a couple of local cable shows, my venture and book titled Grief to Grace was born.

None of it was intentional. There was never a plan for what was next or how I would proceed as time went on. I began to share my story and the book with those closest to me. Slowly, others were contacting me to get their own copy. During that time I began counseling and was part of the pastoral care team at my church. Having completed my Master of Arts degree in Counseling after my cancer diagnosis and subsequent surgeries, I felt that counseling was a good way to utilize my skills and help others. I also created curriculum while at the church to train lay counselors and used that and other material for those who needed support. The church was another catalyst to sharing my story and getting word out about the book. When I left my position at the church I wanted to continue to offer services through my own business, Grief to Grace. Fortunately I had friends and colleagues in support of my endeavors and was able to have office space and find clients. I wanted the business Grief to Grace to be an avenue to share my story and to help others to heal emotionally and spiritually from what I had been educated about, experienced and had experience dealing with in others.

When you are told you don't have long to live, it changes your perspective and life focus. Since I had no idea when my health would deteriorate to the point of no return, life for me personally and professionally is living in a teetering existence of the unknown. It took time to find peace over living in the unknown, but as I continued to realize what my life purpose was I eventually came to the conclusion that diagnosis or not, life is a continual series of the unknown for all of us. As time has passed, I have evolved personally and professionally and I have sharpened my business skills. I've grown my business and learned a great deal simply by asking, seeking and trying different things. I have failed at many things along the way, but continue to remember that as long as I keep learning and do not give up it's all worth it. I also stay committed to continue on by other's comments to me about being encouraged and inspired by what I am doing. I regularly seek new business techniques and ideas from others, especially those who have attained success and met their professional goals. Some of the guests on Your Story Matters show offer great insight about business, that I am fortunate to get first hand.

Along the journey so far I made a couple commitments to myself. One is to share my knowledge and wisdom that I have learned as an entrepreneur with others, whether I am paid for my services or as benevolence. While I agree that we all must know our worth and establish boundaries when sharing and giving it, I also think we should each give freely when we are able to. I believe we can all help each other in this way. The other commitment is to not spend large amounts of money on joining business groups, advertising and workshops. I realized over the first couple years of my endeavors that I spent a great deal of money on things that did not offer me an adequate return on investment. Lastly, I committed to monitoring my time with others. I was initially spending a great deal of time at meetings, networking and calling and emailing others. Again, I found that my efforts and time spent were not provided the return on my investment that I needed.

What I learned was very important. Investing myself in people, connecting online and in person, learning about them and their business, encouraging them and supporting their endeavors is what works magic for me. I have tons of wonderful and amazing connections and contacts all over the world. Most of the guests on the show are found via word of mouth as are listeners to the show. I have developed many friendships from an initial relationship with a colleague. The valuable sharing and learning that has taken place has been incredible. Everyday I am so excited about what is next (or who) and how that will positively impact my life both personally and professionally.

Although my initial business focus was counseling, since I have a degree in counseling and experience in working with various individuals and businesses, I have expanded and included career coaching, small and non-profit business consulting and training. I have also promoted my story and my book as a core focus of what my mission is. Both my personal and professional experiences along my journey over the past six years have brought me to a place of awareness of my life purpose and calling. I know that if I do nothing else, sharing my story and what I have learned is my purpose. I know that a big part of the calling in my life is to encourage and inspire others in any way that will be most effective. I eventually added Your Story Matters Publishing as a subsidiary of my business. I helped a friend write and publish her story and now have created this book to help others to begin thinking through their own story, it's significance and the positive effect it can have on others. I am not calling myself a publisher, but rather a story sharer!

In the midst of my business activities I often happened upon a person or opportunity that helped me to go further in what I was doing. So many great opportunities to share my story and learn about being an entrepreneur have come to me. A significant opportunity during a meeting I was at was one of them. A colleague mentioned hosting a radio show herself and suggested I do a show about my story. I really did not think I could do that or that I would have enough material to do a regular show. But once again I felt a stirring within me that told me I should at least try and pursue this to see where it may lead.

I am so thankful that she suggested this and connected me to an online radio station, where I first launched Your Story Matters show. Though I had a great deal of learning to do and many bumps in the road, the way the show has evolved has been a true blessing. The first two years there were 83,000 listeners worldwide! That meant that many, many people heard stories of others that had the potential to encourage and inspire them! At the same time, I was greatly rewarded for all my hard work and efforts by having the opportunity to connect with and hear these amazing stories from awesome people. As of this writing I continue to share stories of encouragement, hope, faith and more on Your Story Matters show and I have no way to tell what incredible opportunities will come next. I do know, that as long as I am here... the show will go on!

During this journey I have been encouraged by others, many, many times, when I thought I could not keep doing all this, or felt like perhaps I wasn't having the biggest impact that I could. But, I have realized that A) whether what I do by sharing my story and others affects one or thousands, it is important and needed and B) what I am doing and hoping to achieve is a part of my life purpose and it matters! I wanted to list all those people along the journey so far who have been a catalyst for Your Story Matters to go on, but I fear I will accidentally leave someone out. So to all of you, and you know who you are, that have helped encourage me, teach me, support me and challenged me... THANK YOU! You are a part of an important mission to make a better world by sharing our stories!

The story so far, of course, would not be complete if I didn't share some of my challenges along the journey. My biggest critic has been myself! Sometimes I felt like what I was doing just wasn't good enough or did not have enough value. It took awhile, after hearing positive feedback and having others encourage me, for ME to believe I was doing something good. Not perfect by any means, but worthy for sure. And then there is the other big challenge, those who do not believe in what I am doing and/or are unfairly critical of me. Sometimes it seems the harder I try, the more effort I put forth and the BETTER my mission is coming along the more naysayers I come across. But alas, like my life story, this is only a bump along the road that I understand as being par for the course. There is no perfect endeavor that is always running smoothly and without challenges, even if the challenges are other people being unsupportive. I was reminded more than once along this journey that I DO have what's necessary to press on during adversity of any kind. The ability to persevere is a big part of my story! Learning from my own story about my own strengths, weakness and vulnerabilities has been pivotal in following my dreams.

What I learned in telling my own story and sharing it was that *my* story matters. My life experiences matter to many as I share the wisdom I have gained. By telling my story, I have encouraged and inspired many, and that has been an amazing and humbling experience for me. As I wrote my story for my children, reflected on my life and then told my story in public, I experienced a powerful feeling of being valuable and necessary as a part of the world. When others come to me and tell me my story encouraged them to have hope or to not feel so alone, ashamed or worthless, I feel deeply touched. I have come to understand that my life experiences have such power because they help others in many different ways. That was very healing for me, to know that all my pain and heartache throughout my life was for a purpose that I never understood. And today I encourage others to share their life experiences by asking them "What's Your Story"?

I am not going to tell anyone that discovering your life purpose is easy. Depending on what your purpose is, living it out may not be easy either! Nor is learning from and healing from your story. And of course sometimes sharing your story is not easy or comfortable. It is up to you to determine how important it is. It is up to you to find the courage, the will and the motivation. But if you need some help along the way, I hope you will reach out to me!

I am thankful for what I learned along the journey from Grief to Grace to Your Story Matters...

- I did not have a plan about sharing my story or even a vision of what path it would lead me on, but rather I had a whole lot of faith and desire to be obedient to what I believed God called me to do

- Initially I had to overcome a great deal of feeling uncomfortable to step out of the box, put myself out there, and take risks

- Some of my initial willingness to do what I was doing (sharing my story) was the boldness I justified by thinking that the doctors were correct and I would not live long

- I learned to walk in faith and humility each time I asked to be allowed to speak and share my story and/or do a book signing and then to be able to shake off any feelings of discouragement when I was told 'no'

- Although I initially did not understand what the purpose was for sharing my story, I was able to recognize the continual confirmation that I should proceed

- Being at peace with my story, who I was and where I had come from allowed me to be free of expectations of others liking me, agreeing with me or believing in me

- The first time I was told how "amazing and inspiring" I was felt uncomfortable, but I learned over time that left over shame was preventing me from accepting that, although flawed, I am a blessing created by God for a plan and a purpose

- For every word of discouragement I received, there were ten times more the amount of words of encouragement and gratefulness for my willingness to share my story

- For every judgmental attitude I was confronted with, there were ten times the attitude of acceptance and willingness to be open to what I experienced and learned

- While observing others who were attempting to positively impact others I learned the importance of being authentic in my endeavors

- As I felt my true purpose and destiny coming together I was able to stop struggling with the "what if's" and "if only's"

- As I observed and received confirmation of the lives touched via sharing my story, I was able to realize the bigger opportunity to positively impact many more than my immediate circle

- I was able to recognize and receive the gift of healing and freedom when I realized that all I had been through and the challenges before me were all meant to be for the purpose of encouraging and inspiring others through my story

- While initially feeling insecure and vulnerable in speaking, I was able to do it again and again as I gave myself permission to just be me

- Whenever I felt discouraged I reminded myself of all the things in my story that I had overcome and how I had persevered despite overwhelming odds

- I was able to accept and be at peace that if I did not have another day tomorrow, today was enough and I had given my all and left a legacy behind of teaching others the power of healing from shame and guilt and the importance of our stories

- I discovered that the things I desperately wanted to leave behind for my children were not as necessary or valuable as sharing my story with them or encouraging them to learn from and share their own

- When I began to live my purpose I began to experience: amazing opportunities, connecting with great people and having clarity in my life

Addendum~

Vision Board Exercise

I have included the following exercise as yet another tool to look at your story and create a visual for you to set your intentions based on what you have learned and experienced in your life.

1) **Look** back at the past year and answer accordingly:
What mistakes have I made- ones I had control over

What was life **happening-** things I had no control over

What were the most painful, sad or depressing **events**

What I did in response to the above

Why I responded in the way that I did

What **patterns** of behaviors prevented me from living better and reaching my goals?

What **keys** did you learn doing step 1: (i.e. I learned I responded inappropriately and/or as I have done so in the past)

2) **Look** back as far back as you can remember and answer
   accordingly:

What agreements did I make from childhood on about myself (i.e.
I am worthless, I am not as smart as people who succeed etc.)

Why have I made these agreements and carried them with me?
(has someone or   something caused me to believe certain things?)

How have the negative agreements I have carried about myself
affected me reaching my goals?

What **keys** did you learn doing step 2: (i.e. I learned that I have a choice about what I believe about myself, I can change my negative agreements to positive ones)

3) **Look** back over the past year and determine **what worked and did not work**

What took too much **time** (should have ended sooner or not had so much time invested)

Why did I allow myself to spend too much time with this person or project, what was driving me to continuing doing something that was not working for me?

What things or relationships did I 'fall' into unintentionally and **Why**

What **keys** did you learn doing step 3: (i.e. I learned that I have the option to make better choices about how I spend my time, etc.)

4) **Look** back over the past year and ask yourself how you spent
   your time

What took the most time: my personal life, professional life or
being involved in others lives

How did I balance my time taking care of my personal needs, family needs, financial needs, etc.

Did my time spent above work towards **reaching my goals**?

How did I spend my time vs. how did I want to spend my time?

What **keys** did you learn doing step 4: (i.e. I learned I spent too much time on x and not enough on y, etc.)

5) **What** talents, skills and passions do I have that I would like to spend my time doing?

What do I feel happiest doing?

Why would doing what I am good at and passionate about be a good thing?

How could doing what I am good at and passionate about help others?

What **keys** did you learn doing step 5: (i.e time is important to consider; including dollar value for my time and what time I have available based on my priorities)

What words and/or pictures will complete my '**vision**' for my future? (the idea of the board is to have printed words and pictures describing your vision for your life)

Does my vision include both my wants & needs?

How can I balance having my wants and needs met, and am I clear about both?

What **keys** did you learn doing step 6: (i.e. at the core of what I need and want I need to feel; secure, confident, etc.)

7) **What** steps can I take to begin the process of making my vision happen?

Am I ready to move forward, have I let go of unresolved issues of the past?

Is there anything holding me back from working towards my goals

Do I have support in place from others for; feedback, encouragement, etc.

Have I been very clear about what I want?

The outcome of working on my own vision board is as follows: remember that your vision is unique to you and there is no 'wrong' vision to have...

At the core of my 'vision' are my key life words; LOVE (see 1 Corinthians 13:4-7 NIV), PURPOSE, HUMILITY, CONFIDENCE, and GRATITUDE. Surrounding my core words are images to represent; motherly love- my children, money- being debt free, investing and giving, travel- including a mission trip and speaking/ training, good health- taking care of my body, mind and soul, a beach cottage, romantic love, tea time, spa time, and volunteering

We must be INTENTIONAL in order for our vision to evolve into reality... ♥

~ Angela

We invite you to subscribe to Your Story Matters on iTunes at
http://itunes.apple.com/us/podcast/your-story-matters.-you-matter./id491630182

You may also listen to prior shows and find guest information at
http://yourstorymatters.net/category/interviews/inspiring-stories

- If you or someone you know of has a story of encouragement and inspiration to share
- You would like Angela to speak at your event, or to your group or organization
- You would like information about Angela conducting a workshop based on the book
- You are positively impacted by one of the stories

We ask that you let us know by using the contact form at the website or email
info@yourstorymatters.net

If you need counseling , coaching or referrals to appropriate services please contact us. Your Story Matters is committed to providing the best possible resources. You are not alone! There is hope!

What others are saying about Your Story Matters…

Serendipity! Was wondering what I was going to listen to on a long road trip - can't think of anything better than Angela Schaefers- Your Story Matters podcast! Sweet! - Jim West http://www.leaderswest.com

Stories are the foundation of great communication. Keep sharing and inspiring Angela, the ripples you make turn into lasting vibrations! - Victor Sinclair http://positiveimperative.com/

Angela of Your Story Matters continues to encourage and empower me, through the challenges to keep sharing my story. On an ongoing basis Angela is there to say - Lee Your Story Matters, You Matter. - Lee Horbachewski http://simpleeserene.com/

Your Story Matters You Matter

Contact Us!

Inquire about Angela speaking at your event or to your group, writing for you or providing individual or group training or coaching. You may use the contact form at Your Story Matters website www.yourstorymatters.net or contact us via:

Email: info@yourstorymatters.net

Phone: 877-272-2481

Media inquiries are welcome. Ms. Schaefers bio is available via the website.

18598053R00072

Made in the USA
Lexington, KY
14 November 2012